Photography At Auction Digest

volume ii

Designed by AXF Design
Copyright 2020
Edition: 1
ISBN: 9781655544378

This book contains data compiled over a twelve month period using results from photography sales by the three largest auction houses in the world: Christie's, Phillips, and Sotheby's. These auctions houses were specifically chosen not only for their reputations as leaders at auction, but for their consistent commitment to the sale of photography and repeated record breaking sales of photographic prints. This book is concerned exclusively with photographic sales at auction; private sales are not included as they are largely unverifiable.

Photography At Auction is an industry-specific website regarding news and notices of photographic sales from the elite auction houses as well as relevant industry news, find out more at
www.photographyatauction.com

All information correct at time of publication.

References can be found at the back of this book

Contents

Introduction

The Valuation Formula

Though photography is a diverse field with any number of subjects, cameras and methods of processing, since its inception into the auction world in the mid-19th century there has grown a particular set of distinctions for valuing a photograph. Though certainly not a strict set of rules, this general 'valuation formula' is a good indicator of a print's value. This formula consisting of four major factors:

Reputation

A print made by an unknown photographer, however beautiful, is rarely going to sell for more than a few hundred dollars. Like any art practice, reputation is everything, and the sale of a well-known artist tends to attract more bids. Successful artists are those who have been practitioners for a number of years with a catalogue of experience and accolades behind them. They are tried and trusted artists, who buyers recognise. With this in mind, the more famous a photographer is, the more likely their images are to sell well at auction. Examples of this include Edward Weston ($1.6m Sotheby's New York 2008), Man Ray ($3.1m Christie's Paris 2017) and Richard Avedon ($1.1m Christie's Paris 2010), all of whom have been recognised names for decades, becoming masters of their fields and lauded long after their deaths.

Provenance

Connected to reputation is a print's history. Is it a well-known print? Was it exhibited in national galleries? Who previously owned the print? All these factors contribute to the value of the piece. Conversely, the fewer connections the artwork has to its artist the less desirable the print becomes. For example, if the print was made after the death of the artist it will be considered less valuable, because it lacks the provenance of being created by the artists themselves.

Editioning

Editioning is key. Art forms such as painting command higher hammer prices thanks to their rarefied nature - generally they are one-of-a-kind with very few, if any, other copies of the painting. This largely explains why photography was considered a bad investment during its early days of endless reproduction. Today, however, photographs are limited to a set number of editions, meaning that the photographer decides how many reproductions of their image are going to be produced and annotates each image with its placement in the collection, i.e. the first print of ten editions means that there are nine other copies of that print, it's placement as number one also contributes to its value. This discipline has significantly contributed to photography's desirability as an investment, and is reflected in many auction results. Andreas Gursky's 1999 work

Rhine II is the most expensive photograph to sell at auction selling for $4,338,500 (Christie's New York, 2011) and is edition one of only six. This also explains why famous works by significantly better-known artists may sell for less, with hundreds of copies out there; their reputation is not enough to guarantee a high hammer price.

Uniqueness

One of the great elements of auctioning is unpredictability, a work of art can hit all the previous qualifiers and fail to shift on auction day, or better yet, a piece could have no other qualities and still raise millions in bids. This can all be down to the uniqueness of the print. In 2011, a photograph by an unknown artist sold at auction for $2.3 million (Brian Lebel's Old West Show) for two reasons: the image was one of the only confirmed portraits of famed outlaw and historic figure Billy the Kid, and the image was created using tin-type processing; a unique form of image-making by which the photograph is directly exposed on to tin and becomes the print itself - a one-of-a-kind image which cannot be reprinted through the use of 'negatives'. Both features made the photograph a very unique sale, and resulted in one of the most expensive images to sell at auction.

This formula isn't ironclad, and ultimately what sells on any given day is whatever the buyers want at that time, making photography at auction an unpredictable and compelling industry.

Essays

January 2019

Looking Back at Photography's Place at Auction in 2018

Photography has had a seemingly consistent upward trajectory since its arrival as a commodity over 160 years ago, and though hammer prices are drastically smaller than those seen at auction for paintings, the photographic print is fast catching up. In 2005, an auction took place in New York, in which a photograph sold for over $1 million - just over 150 years since a photograph was first sold at auction. Compare that with painting's vast history as a commodity, and it may come as a surprise to discover that the first painting to sell for over a million dollars sold in the 1970s.

While the most expensive photograph to sell at auction, Andreas Gursky's *Rhine II* for $4.3 million (Christie's New York, 2011), trails significantly behind the most expensive painting, Da Vinci's *Salvator Mundi* for $450.3 million (Christie's New York, 2017), photography's presence as a commodity continues to gather pace.

In 2017, four photographs sold at auction for over $1 million, including Man Ray's *Noire et Blanche* for $3.1 million (Christie's Paris), which entered the top ten list of the most expensive photographs to sell at auction. This was a world record for the artist, in a year that saw his work enter the chart for the first time, with two outstanding sales.

In 2018, Helmut Newton entered the top fifty for the first time, with a world record sale of *Panoramic Nude with Gun, Villa d'Este, Como* for $981,884 (Phillips London), along with a print by Diane Arbus, whose *Identical twins, Roselle, N.J.* for $732,500 (Christie's New York) was work by only the second female to feature in the list. These additions, in quick succession, show that tastes in photography continue to develop, though a taste for analogue photographs continues to persist.

Of the ten most expensive sales in 2018, all of them were captured through analogue photography, and though digital prints have been consigned and sold under the hammer, analogue photography is by far the most desirable means of image-making, certainly as far as investors are concerned.

Though there were no astronomical sales in 2018, the three elite auction houses of Christie's, Phillips and Sotheby's realised a combined total of $47.6 million in sales from 25 photography auctions.

This article was also printed in the *Royal Photographic Society's* 2019 *Analogue* magazine.

January 2019

Fact Checking: The Most Expensive Photographs Sold at Auction

During research for volume one of the **Digest** it became apparent that the previously published lists of the most expensive photographs to be sold at auction are wrong.

These lists can be found all over the internet with any number of inaccuracies, including Gustave Le Gray's **The Great Wave, Sete** almost exclusively reported across the internet as selling for $625 more than its actual hammer price, or Gilbert & George's **Red Morning (Hell)** which sold for $36,489 more than its reported value in US dollars. Judging from the disparities it seems that some publications have rounded results up or miscalculated currency exchange on the day of sale.

Where possible we set about finding the original hammer prices as listed by the auction houses, before calculating their worth in US dollars according to historic registers of currency exchanges on the day of sale. This resulted in a restructuring of the top 50 list of most expensive photographs to be sold at auction, shifting Wolfgang Tillman's **Freishwimmer 84** from 41st in the list down to 43rd, while Man Ray's **Noire et Blanche** moved up from 14th position to 8th.

It is clear how easily false reporting can become fact, and how much content on the internet is regurgitated.

After this research Photography At Auction's list of the 50 most expensive photography sales was revised and edited and consequently became the only known definitive catalogue of the 50 prints. Since last year's publication that has been some additions and, as such, the list has been edited and republished in this book.

March 2019

What The Winter Auctions Mean For Photography

As we slip into March we shake off the vestiges of 2018 and welcome the promise of spring. As far as photography auctions are concerned we are at the cusp of some of the biggest photography auctions in the calendar, so it seems an appropriate time to reflect on what has come so far.

The start of 2019 has provided scant winter offerings with only three auctions concerning photography, all of which were mixed-media auctions with two held online. Without Sotheby's there would have been no activity for photography this season as all three auctions were hosted by the house. It has, however, provided a little preview into photography's current position.

At ***The Fine Art Society: 142 Years on New Bond Street*** Sotheby's brought together 312 lots of furniture, illustrations, sketches, paintings and a handful of photographs. Photography made up less than 2% of the consignments, consisting of un-editioned works by relatively undervalued artists (compared with the usual marquee names like Cecil Beaton and Man Ray), but saw 40% of those lots sell for over their highest estimates. At the close of sale, 2 photographs remained unsold of 71 unsold lots. Though this is hardly a news-worthy item it shows that even in a largely pre-20th century auction with somewhat obscure photographic offerings, there is still a taste for photography, be it for their subject or historical value, such as a collection of 39 prints of 1851 The Great Exhibition, which sold for £1,125 (£325 above its top estimate).

A similar story was the case for the second auction, **Erotic: Passion & Desire**, an annual online auction that saw 67 lots available with only 9 photographs. Together the photographic lots brought in £45,000 (10%) to a combined sales total of £446,375. This time photography lots were a combination of black and white and colour, with the highest selling print (£23,750) created as recently as 2017.

Finally **Now! Online,** another annual online auction, saw 40 photographs available from 255 lots (15%) going up against contemporary paintings (the highest selling genre at auction). Together photography contributed €146,875 (just under 12%) to the combined sales total of €1,259,250. For a category that is still one of the smallest and least funded departments, and one of the newest art forms, photography is proving itself as a steady seller. With the most anticipated auctions of spring approaching photography could yet prove its headline-grabbing value too.

August 2019

How Photography is Performing at Auction (so far)

In the summer of 2018 Christie's, Phillips and Sotheby's had hosted 14 photography-specific auctions between them. Helmut Newton's **Panoramic Nude with Gun** had sold in May for $981,884 making it a world record for the artist and the most expensive print that year.

Fast-forward a year and the photography-specific auction tally is down (11) but the records are up.

Though auction houses have restrained the number of photography auctions they have hosted so far this year, their consignments have been more successful. Already this year photography has outpaced last year's number of record-breaking sales with two prints sold for over $1 million and three entered into the list of the top 50 Most Expensive Photographs Sold at Auction.

Of the three most expensive sales so far this year, Edward Weston's **Shell (Nautilus)** was the cheapest at $674,977 (Christie's London), just over $300,000 less than last year's most expensive sale. The print was Weston's fifth to enter the top 50 joining El Lissitzky who, this year, entered the top 50 for the first time.

Lissitzky's *Self-Portrait ('The Constructor')* smashed the artist's world record at the same auction as Weston's print (Christie's London) in March by reaching a hammer price of $1.2 million and placing 33rd in the top 50 list.

It is Helmut Newton, however, who has had the best performance so far this year, beating his best record set only last year with a $1.8 million sale at Phillips (New York) in April – over $800,000 more than his previous record.

With Helmut Newton entering the top 50 for the first time last year and El Lissitsky entering for the first time this year, it would appear buyers consider photography attractive enough to take a punt on. And though photography auctions have decreased this year along with photography-inclusive sales, the numbers suggest that photography continues to be a worthy investment.

December 2019

Photography's $67 Million Year

As the international art market teeters on the edge of a downturn, photography is enjoying a steady climb upwards.

It may have been two years since a standout sale broke into the list of the top ten most expensive photographs and nine years since the number one record was broken, the overall view of photography at auction is favourable. In the last decade, there have been twenty-five photographs sold at auction for over $1 million, with two sold this year alone.

Using the Top 50 Most Expensive Photographs Sold At Auction as a source for comparison, the last ten years have shown a consistent stream of record-breaking sales. Every year since the turn of the decade at least two photographs have entered the top 50 list, with many artists entering the hallowed database for the first time.

In 2017 Man Ray entered the Top 50 for the first time with two photographs (*Portrait of a Tearful Woman* for over $2.1 million and *Noire et Blanche* for over $3.1 million), proceeded in 2018 with the entry of Helmut Newton for the first time (with *Panoramic Nude with Gun, Villa d'este, Como* at $981,884) and Diane Arbus (with *Identical twins, Roselle, N.J. 1966* for $732,500) as only the second female artist to enter the list.

2019 has continued this trend with a global auction record for El Lissitzky whose *Self-Portrait ('The Constructor')* sold for over $1.2 million and saw the early 20th century artist enter the list for the first time. 2019 saw three entries into the Top 50 List, from the aforementioned El Lissitzky, as well as Helmut Newton and Edward Weston.

The most expensive photograph of the year was Newton's *Sie Kommen, Paris (Dressed and Naked)*, which sold at Phillips New York for over $1.8 million – over $800,000 more than the most expensive print the previous year (also a Helmut Newton image), in an auction that saw a combined sales total of over $10.4 million - $6 million more than the highest sales total of 2018.

In 2018 twenty-five auctions resulted in a combined sales total of over $47.6 million. In 2019 twenty-five auctions resulted in a combined sales total of over $67 million. Though this upturn in prices is a small snapshot of photography sales, it does reflect a wider trend particularly as more auction records are broken each year. So perhaps as buyers look to diversify their investments within the art market, the long-regarded alternative art form of photography is proving to be a successful alternative investment too?

Auctions

6 March 2019
Masterpieces of Design and Photography
Christie's London

Sales total (inc. buyer's premium) **£6,421,500**

Most Expensive Lot: Lot 114
Title: *Self-Portrait ('The Constructor')*
Artist: El Lissitzky
Estimate: £800,000-£1,200,000
Price Realised: £947,250 ($1,240,897)

2nd Most Expensive Lot: Lot 102
Title: *Shell (Nautilus)*
Artist: Edward Weston
Estimate: £500,000-£700,000
Price Realised: £515,250 ($674,977)

3rd Most Expensive Lot: Lot 109
Title: *Mailander Dom (innen), Mailand*
Artist: Thomas Struth
Estimate: £180,000-£250,000
Price Realised: £419,250 ($549,217)

2 April 2019

Daydreaming: Photographs from the Goldstein Collection
Christie's New York

Sales total (inc. buyer's premium) **$1,614,750**

Most Expensive Lot: Lot 44
Title: Dovima with Elephants, Evening Dress by Dior, Cirque d'Hiver, Paris, 1955
Artist: Richard Avedon
Estimate: $350,000-$550,000
Price Realised: $615,000

2nd Most Expensive Lot: Lot 7
Title: *Harlequin Dress (Lisa Fonssagrives-Penn), NY, 1950*
Artist: Irving Penn
Estimate: $200,000-$300,000
Price Realised: $325,000

3rd Most Expensive Lot: Lot 45
Title: *Marilyn Monroe, actress, New York City, May 6, 1957*
Artist: Richard Avedon
Estimate: $70,000-$100,000
Price Realised: $100,000

2 April 2019

The Face of the Century: Photographs from a Private Collection
Christie's New York

Sales total (inc. buyer's premium) **$1,812,000**

Most Expensive Lot: Lot 188
Title: *Self Portrait with Wife and Models, Paris, 1981*
Artist: Helmut Newton
Estimate: $40,000-$60,000
Price Realised: $100,000

2nd Most Expensive Lot: Lot 190
Title: *Tied-Up Torso, Ramatuelle, 1980*
Artist: Helmut Newton
Estimate: $50,000-$70,000
Price Realised: $100,000

3rd Most Expensive Lot: Lot 133
Title: *Rayograph (Kiki Silhouette, Positive), 1922-1938*
Artist: Man Ray
Estimate: $100,000-$150,000
Price Realised: $87,500

2 April 2019
Photographs
Christie's New York

Sales total (inc. buyer's premium) **$3,511,750**

Most Expensive Lot: Lot 372
Title: *Lestnitsa (steps), 1929*
Artist: Alexander Rodchenko
Estimate: $150,000-$250,000
Price Realised: $281,250

2nd Most Expensive Lot: Lot 359
Title: *A family on their lawn one Sunday in Westchester, N.Y. 1968*
Artist: Diane Arbus
Estimate: $250,000-$350,000
Price Realised: $275,000

3rd Most Expensive Lot: Lot 384
Title: *The Family, Luzzara, Italy, 1953*
Artist: Paul Strand
Estimate: $200,000-$300,000
Price Realised: $250,000

4 April 2019
Passion & Humanity: The Susie Tompkins Buell Collection
Phillips New York

Sales total (inc. buyer's premium) **$2,608,625**

Most Expensive Lot: Lot 12
Title: *Circus Tent*
Artist: Edward Weston
Estimate: $400,000-$600,000
Price Realised: $788,000

2nd Most Expensive Lot: Lot 8
Title: *Telephone wires, Mexico*
Artist: Tina Modotti
Estimate: $250,000-$350,000
Price Realised: $692,000

3rd Most Expensive Lot: Lot 15
Title: *Heavy Roses, Voulangis, France*
Artist: Edward Steichen
Estimate: $400,000-$600,000
Price Realised: $524,000

4 April 2019
Photographs
Phillips New York

Sales total (inc. buyer's premium) **$10,490,875**

Most Expensive Lot: Lot 85
Title: *Sie Kommen, Paris (Dressed and Naked)*
Artist: Helmut Newton
Estimate: $600,000-$800,000
Price Realised: $1,820,000

2nd Most Expensive Lot: Lot 74
Title: *Tsavo East (early '60's), (as Brör Blixen knew it in the '20's + '30's), West of Daka Dima/ near the Tiva for The End of the Game/ Last Word from Paradise*
Artist: Peter Beard
Estimate: $150,000-$250,000
Price Realised: $187,500

3rd Most Expensive Lot: Lot 141
Title: *US 285, New Mexico*
Artist: Robert Frank
Estimate: $25,000-$35,000
Price Realised: $187,500

5 April 2019

Photographs
Sotheby's New York

Sales total (inc. buyer's premium) **$4,035,625**

Most Expensive Lot: Lot 13
Title: *Pelikan Tinte*
Artist: El Lissitzky
Estimate: $300,000-$500,000
Price Realised: $459,000

2nd Most Expensive Lot: Lot 22
Title: *Black and White Vogue Cover (Jean Patchett, New York)*
Artist: Irving Penn
Estimate: $150,000-$250,000
Price Realised: $187,500

3rd Most Expensive Lot: Lot 102
Title: *Aspens, Northern New Mexico*
Artist: Ansel Adams
Estimate: $150,000-$250,000
Price Realised: $187,500

2-7 May 2019

Weegee Photographs: The Elastic Lens
Christie's Online

Sales total (inc. buyer's premium) **$53,625**

Most Expensive Lot: Lot 2
Title: *Jumping on Beach, c. 1955*
Artist: Weegee
Estimate: $6,000-$8,000
Price Realised: $12,500

2nd Most Expensive Lot: Lot 15
Title: *Lingerie distortion (standing), c.1955*
Artist: Weegee
Estimate: $6,000-$8,000
Price Realised: $3,500

3rd Most Expensive Lot: Lot 16
Title: *Lingerie distortion (seated), c.1955*
Artist: Weegee
Estimate: $6,000-$8000
Price Realised: $2,250

16 May 2019
Photographs
Sotheby's London

Sales total (inc. buyer's premium) **£966,875**

Most Expensive Lot: Lot 73
Title: *Loliondo Lion Charge, for the end of the game / Last Word From Paradise, 1964*
Artist: Peter Beard
Estimate: £60,000-£80,000
Price Realised: £75,000

2nd Most Expensive Lot: Lot 94
Title: *Estelle Lefebure, Karen Alexander, Rachel Williams, Linda Evangelista, Tatjana Patzt, Christy Burlington, Santa Monica, California, USA, 1988*
Artist: Peter Lindbergh
Estimate: £60,000-£80,000
Price Realised: £75,000

3rd Most Expensive Lot: Lot 20
Title: *Dovima with Elephants, Evening Dress by Dior, Cirque D'Hiver, Paris, 1955*
Artist: Richard Avedon
Estimate: £30,000-£50,000
Price Realised: £50,000

16 May 2019
Photographs
Phillips London

Sales total (inc. buyer's premium) **£1,849,188**

Most Expensive Lot: Lot 40
Title: *La Priere (Prayer)*
Artist: Man Ray
Estimate: £50,000-£70,000
Price Realised: £100,000

2nd Most Expensive Lot: Lot 21
Title: *16h 28m/-60°*
Artist: Thomas Ruff
Estimate: £50,000-£70,000
Price Realised: £56,250

3rd Most Expensive Lot: Lot 37
Title: *Self-Portrait*
Artist: Stanislaw Ignacy Witkiewicz (Witkacy)
Estimate: £30,000-£50,000
Price Realised: £50,000

7 June 2019
Artist, Icon, Inspiration: Women in Photography
Phillips New York

Sales total (inc. buyer's premium) **£985,250**

Most Expensive Lot: Lot 65
Title: *Migrant Mother, Nipomo, California*
Artist: Dorothea Lange
Estimate: $70,000-$90,000
Price Realised: $87,500

2nd Most Expensive Lot: Lot 15
Title: *Untitled (man smoking) from Kitchen Table Series*
Artist: Carrie Mae Weems
Estimate: $25,000-$35,000
Price Realised: $70,000

3rd Most Expensive Lot: Lot 82
Title: *Relevance, Supposition, Connection, Viewpoint, Evidence from Questions*
Artist: Anne Collier
Estimate: $50,000-$60,000
Price Realised: $62,5000

19 June 2019

Icons of Glamour & Style: The Constantiner Collection
Christie's Paris

Sales total (inc. buyer's premium) **€2,643,625**

Most Expensive Lot: Lot 27
Title: *Dovima with Elephants, Evening Dress by Dior, Cirque d'Hiver, Paris, 1955*
Artist: Richard Avedon
Estimate: €250,000-€350000
Price Realised: €262,000

2nd Most Expensive Lot: Lot 42
Title: *Statue of Liberty, 1976-1986*
Artist: Andy Warhol
Estimate: €40,000-€60,000
Price Realised: €212,500

3rd Most Expensive Lot: Lot 20
Title: *Harlequin Dress (Lisa Fonssagrives-Penn), 1950*
Artist: Irving Penn
Estimate: €200,000-€300,000
Price Realised: €200,000

16-24 July 2019

Photographs: New York, New York
Christie's Online

Sales total (inc. buyer's premium) **$76,375**

Most Expensive Lot: Lot 8
Title: *New York (Woman with taxi), 1982*
Artist: Helen Levitt
Estimate: $4000-$6000
Price Realised: $8,750

2nd Most Expensive Lot: Lot 6
Title: *Party, Jukebox, 1940s*
Artist: Weegee
Estimate: $3,000-$5,000
Price Realised: $5,625

3rd Most Expensive Lot: Lot 15
Title: *New York (Children with a broken mirror)*
Artist: Helen Levitt
Estimate: $4,000-$6,000
Price Realised: $5,625

6-17 September 2019
Chris Levine: Be Light
Sotheby's London

Sales total (inc. buyer's premium) **£248,125**

Most Expensive Lot: Lot 5
Title: *Lightness of Being, 2018*
Artist: Chris Levine
Estimate: £70,000-£100,000
Price Realised: £75,000

2nd Most Expensive Lot: Lot 6
Title: *Banksy (3D), 2017*
Artist: Chris Levine
Estimate: £3,000-£5,000
Price Realised: £35,000

3rd Most Expensive Lot: Lot 4
Title: *Kate Moss She's Light (3D), 2013*
Artist: Chris Levine
Estimate: £20,000-£30,000
Price Realised: £25,000

27 September 2019

Contemporary Photographs
Sotheby's New York

Sales total (inc. buyer's premium) **$1,885,375**

Most Expensive Lot: Lot 71
Title: *Untitled Film Still #10*
Artist: Cindy Sherman
Estimate: $120,000-$180,000
Price Realised: $300,000

2nd Most Expensive Lot: Lot 13
Title: *Untitled Film Still #45*
Artist: Cindy Sherman
Estimate: $120,000-$180,000
Price Realised: $162,500

3rd Most Expensive Lot: Lot 87
Title: *Large-Maned Lion at Cottar's Camp*
Artist: Peter Beard
Estimate: $40,000-$60,000
Price Realised: $106,250

1 October 2019

Photographs
Phillips New York

Sales total (inc. buyer's premium) **$3,534,000**

Most Expensive Lot: Lot 111
Title: *S.O.S. Starification Object Series (Performalist Self-Portrait with Les William), 1974*
Artist: Hannah Wilke
Estimate: $180,000-$280,000
Price Realised: $225,000

2nd Most Expensive Lot: Lot 54
Title: *Parade, Hoboken, New Jersey, 1955*
Artist: Robert Frank
Estimate: $70,000-$90,000
Price Realised: $162,500

3rd Most Expensive Lot: Lot 68
Title: *Trolley, New Orleans, 1955*
Artist: Robert Frank
Estimate: $50,000-$70,000
Price Realised: $150,000

2 October 2019
Photographs
Christie's New York

Sales total (inc. buyer's premium) **$6,015,000**

Most Expensive Lot: Lot 349
Title: *Panoramic Nude, Woman with Gun, Villa d'Este, Como, 1989*
Artist: Helmut Newton
Estimate: $300,000-$500,000
Price Realised: $399,000

2nd Most Expensive Lot: Lot 140
Title: *From the Radio Tower, Berlin, 1928*
Artist: Laszlo Moholy-Nagy
Estimate: $200,000-$300,000
Price Realised: $275,000

3rd Most Expensive Lot: Lot 343
Title: *World-Class Black Rhino, Aberdare Forest, 1972*
Artist: Peter Beard
Estimate: $40,000-$60,000
Price Realised: $250,000

3 October 2019
Classic Photographs
Sotheby's New York

Sales total (inc. buyer's premium) **$2,382,250**

Most Expensive Lot: Lot 121
Title: *Polka Dots*
Artist: Francesca Woodman
Estimate: $50,000-$70,000
Price Realised: $200,000

2nd Most Expensive Lot: Lot 149
Title: *Floyd Burroughs, A Cotton Sharecropper, Hale County, Alabama*
Artist: Walker Evans
Estimate: $80,000-$120,000
Price Realised: $150,000

3rd Most Expensive Lot: Lot 208
Title: *Tulips*
Artist: Robert Mapplethorpe
Estimate: $80,000-$120,000
Price Realised: $93,750

25 October 2019
Photographs
Phillips London

Sales total (inc. buyer's premium) **£1,655,750**

Most Expensive Lot: Lot 10⁻
Title: *756 elephants in a "misery likes company" formation / destroyed social units from starvation / exceeding carrying capacity / over-population / + mismanagement / TSAVO / @ the Mkomazi border / for The End of the Game / last word from paradise*
Artist: Peter Beard
Estimate: £100,000-£150,000
Price Realised: £212,500

2nd Most Expensive Lot: Lot 43
Title: *The Gardeners of Eden*
Artist: Peter Beard
Estimate: £80,000-£120,000
Price Realised: £100,000

3rd Most Expensive Lot: Lot 46
Title: *Francis Bacon, artist, Paris, April 11*
Artist: Richard Avedon
Estimate: £80,000-£120,000
Price Realised: £81,250

5 November 2019

Photographs
Christie's Paris

Sales total (inc. buyer's premium) **€2,821,875**

Most Expensive Lot: Lot 22
Title: *Marilyn Monroe, actress, New York city, 6 may 1957*
Artist: Richard Avedon
Estimate: €300,000-€500,000
Price Realised: €346,000

2nd Most Expensive Lot: Lot 57
Title: *Le Coq, La Muse Endormie, 1924*
Artist: Constantin Brancusi
Estimate: €50,000-€70,000
Price Realised: €187,000

3rd Most Expensive Lot: Lot 12
Title: *Lavender Glory Poppy, New York, 1968*
Artist: Irving Penn
Estimate: €50,000-€70,000
Price Realised: €137,000

5 November 2019

Photographies
Sotheby's Paris

Sales total (inc. buyer's premium) **€1,512,125**

Most Expensive Lot: Lot 65
Title: *23 Works from Unbewussete Orte (Unconscious Places), 1979-1989*
Artist: Thomas Struth
Estimate: €100,000-€150,000
Price Realised: €125,000

2nd Most Expensive Lot: Lot 64
Title: *Untitled 103, 1983*
Artist: Cindy Sherman
Estimate: €80,000-€120,000
Price Realised: €100,000

3rd Most Expensive Lot: Lot 69
Title: *Bronzino, 2015*
Artist: Wolfgang Tillmans
Estimate: €70,000-€90,000
Price Realised: €87,500

4-14 November 2019
Photographs Online
Sotheby's Paris

Sales total (inc. buyer's premium) **€128,250**

Most Expensive Lot: Lot 1
Title: *Time Exposed, 1991*
Artist: Hiroshi Sugimoto
Estimate: €12,000-€18,000
Price Realised: €18,750

2nd Most Expensive Lot: Lot 6
Title: *Metal, 1928*
Artist: Germaine Krull
Estimate: €10,000-€15,000
Price Realised: €12,500

3rd Most Expensive Lot: Lot 7
Title: *Photographs from around Mexico City, 1903-1919*
Artist: Edmond Hamel
Estimate: €8,000-€12,000
Price Realised: €10,000

23 November – 3 December 2019
Space Photography Online
Sotheby's Online

Sales total (inc. buyer's premium) **$380,250**

Most Expensive Lot: Lot 60
Title: *[Apollo 8] Earthrise, as photographed from the Apollo 8 CM. Vintage Large Format Photograph, 24 Dec 1968*
Artist: William Anders
Estimate: $4,000-$6,000
Price Realised: $60,000

2nd Most Expensive Lot: Lot 214
Title: *UFO sighting. 6 Vintage Photos taken by "Billy" Eduard Albert Meier in Switzerland from 3 March-14 June 1975.*
Artist: "Billy" Eduard Albert Meier
Estimate: $6,000-$9,000
Price Realised: $16,250

3rd Most Expensive Lot: Lot 95
Title: *[Apollo 11] First Footprint on the lunar surface. Vintage NASA "Red Number" Photograph, 20 July 1969*
Artist: Buzz Aldrin [?] (Photographer not listed)
Estimate: $3,000-$5,000
Price Realised: $13,750

10 December 2019

Ansel Adams and the American West: Photographs from the Centre for Creative Photography
Christie's New York

Sales total (inc. buyer's premium) **$1,098,250**

Most Expensive Lot: Lot 41
Title: *Moonrise, Hernandez, New Mexico, 1941*
Artist: Ansel Adams
Estimate: $30,000-$50,000
Price Realised: $75,000

2nd Most Expensive Lot: Lot 3
Title: *Clearing Winter Storm, Yosemite Valley, California, 1938*
Artist: Ansel Adams
Estimate: $30,000-$50,000
Price Realised: $60,000

3rd Most Expensive Lot: Lot 32
Title: *The Tetons and the Snake River, Grand Teton National Park, Wyoming, 1942*
Artist: Ansel Adams
Estimate: $20,000-$30,000
Price Realised: $58,750

2-11 December 2019
Fashion Photo
Christie's Online

Sales total (inc. buyer's premium) **$221,500**

Most Expensive Lot: Lot 8
Title: *Black and White Fashion (with handbag) (Jean Patchett), New York, 1950*
Artist: Irving Penn
Estimate: $60,000-$80,000
Price Realised: $75,000

2nd Most Expensive Lot: Lot 6
Title: *Veruschka, Dress by Kimberly, New York Studio, January, 1967*
Artist: Richard Avedon
Estimate: $20,000-$30,000
Price Realised: $25,000

3rd Most Expensive Lot: Lot 25
Title: *Hat and Five Roses, 1956*
Artist: William Klein
Estimate: $7,000-$9,000
Price Realised: $15,000

Data

Most Expensive Sales

10.

$399,000

Panoramic Nude, Woman with Gun, Villa d'Este,
Como, 1989

Helmut Newton

Photographs, Christie's New York, 2 October 2019

9.

$459,000

Pelikan Tinte

El Lissitzky

Photographs, Sotheby's New York, 5 April 2019

8.

$524,000

Heavy Roses, Voulangis, France

Edward Steichen

Passion & Humanity: The Susie Tompkins Buell Collection,
Phillips New York, 4 April 2019

7.

$549,217

Mailander Dom (innen), Mailand

Thomas Struth

Masterpieces of Design and Photography, Christie's

London, 6 March 2019

6.

$615,000

Dovima with Elephants, Evening Dress by Dior, Cirque d'Hiver, Paris, 1955)

Richard Avedon

Daydreaming: Photographs from the Goldstein Collection,

Christie's New York, 2 April 2019

5.

$674,977

Shell (Nautilus)

Edward Weston

Masterpieces of Design and Photography, Christie's
London, 6 March 2019

4.

$692,000

Telephone wires, Mexico

Tina Modotti

Passion & Humanity: The Susie Tompkins Buell Collection,
Phillips New York, 4 April 2019

3.

$788,000

Circus Tent

Edward Weston

Passion & Humanity: The Susie Tompkins Buell Collection,
Phillips New York, 4 April 2019

2.

$1,240,897

Self-Portrait ('The Constructor')

El Lissitzky

Masterpieces of Design and Photography, Christie's

London, 6 March 2019

1.

$1,820,000

Sie Kommen, Paris (Dressed and Naked)

Helmut Newton

Photographs, Phillips New York, 4 April 2019

Facts & Trends

Trends of 2019

Most common print type: Silver Gelatin Print

Most successful recurring print: *Dovima with Elephant, Evening Dress by Dior, Cirque d'hiver, Paris, 1955,* with three prints selling in the top three most expensive lots in their respective auctions, the most expensive edition of the print sold for $615,000 in April at Christie's New York. The photograph was also the most successful recurring print of 2018.

Most Common Subject: Fashion

Facts & Figures

El Lissitzky's work entered the top 50 most expensive photographs list for the first time this year with *Self-Portrait ('The Constructor')*, which was also the second most expensive print of the year.

World auction records were set for several female photographers this year including Hannah Wilkes, Margaret Bourke-White and Tina Modotti whose *Telephone wires, Mexico* was one of the most expensive prints of the year.

Helmut Newton's *Sie Kommen, Paris (Dressed and Naked)* was not only the most expensive photograph of the year it was also the most expensive lot to ever sell at a Phillips photography auction

Photography Auction with the Highest Sales Total:

Photographs
Phillips New York
4 April 2019
$10,490,875

Photography Auction with Highest Hammer Prices:

Passion & Humanity: The Susie Tompkins Buell Collection
Phillips New York
4 April 2019

Most Prolific Auction House for Photography Auctions:

Christie's: 11
Sotheby's: 8
Phillips: 6

Auction Activity

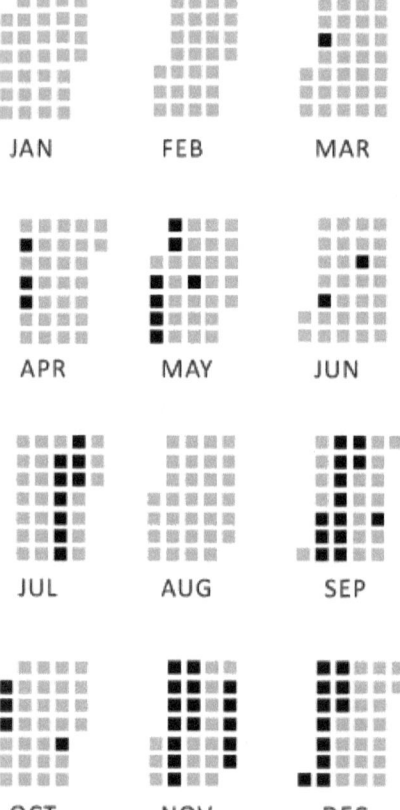

JAN   FEB   MAR

APR   MAY   JUN

JUL   AUG   SEP

OCT   NOV   DEC

Compared with 2018, the photography auctions were fairly evenly spread throughout 2019 with the usual gaps in February and August. However, the first quarter of the year comprised of only one auction in the form of Christie's *Masterpieces of Design and Photography*, which brought in a healthy sales total and some of the highest hammer prices of the year.

April saw the most activity with all three of the elite auction houses hosting photography auctions including *Passion & Humanity: The Susie Tompkins Buell Collection* and *Photographs* both held by Phillips and both bringing in the highest hammer prices of the year and the highest sales total, respectively.

Though the second half of the year appears to have seen more activity regarding photography auctions, four of the five online photography auctions were hosted at the end of the year. These digital auctions usually provide buyers with more affordable and often more contemporary prints and therefore often result in lower sales totals.

There were 25 photography auctions in 2019 including four exclusive photography auctions selling prints from private collections.

Number of Auctions

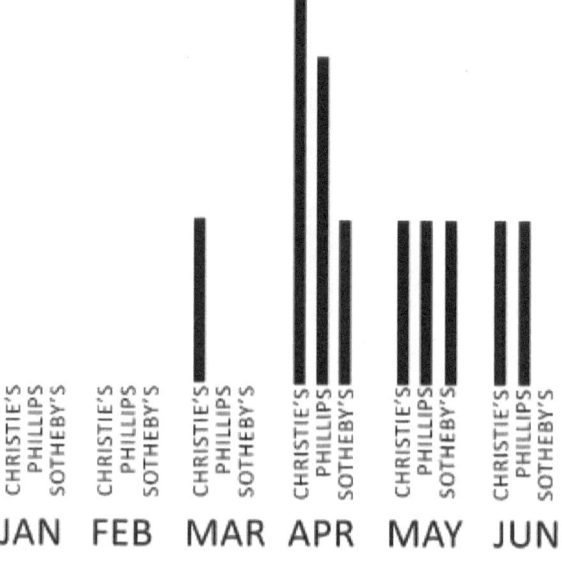

CHRISTIE'S
PHILLIPS
SOTHEBY'S
JAN

CHRISTIE'S
PHILLIPS
SOTHEBY'S
FEB

CHRISTIE'S
PHILLIPS
SOTHEBY'S
MAR

CHRISTIE'S
PHILLIPS
SOTHEBY'S
APR

CHRISTIE'S
PHILLIPS
SOTHEBY'S
MAY

CHRISTIE'S
PHILLIPS
SOTHEBY'S
JUN

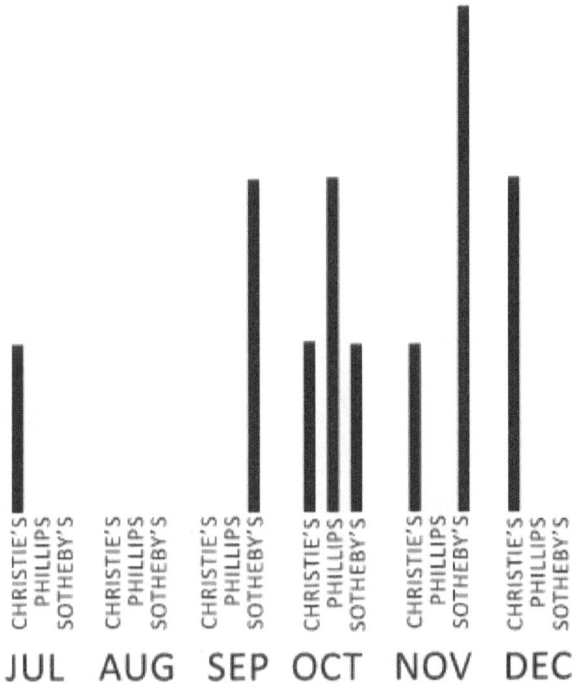

CHRISTIE'S
PHILLIPS
SOTHEBY'S

CHRISTIE'S
PHILLIPS
SOTHEBY'S

CHRISTIE'S
PHILLIPS
SOTHEBY'S

CHRISTIE'S
PHILLIPS
SOTHEBY'S

CHRISTIE'S
PHILLIPS
SOTHEBY'S

CHRISTIE'S
PHILLIPS
SOTHEBY'S

JUL   AUG   SEP   OCT   NOV   DEC

Christie's held the highest number of auctions in 2019 with 11 sales. Christie's and Sotheby's tied on the highest number of photography auctions in one month, with 3 each in April and November. Phillips held the fewest number of auctions, with 6.

Sales Totals

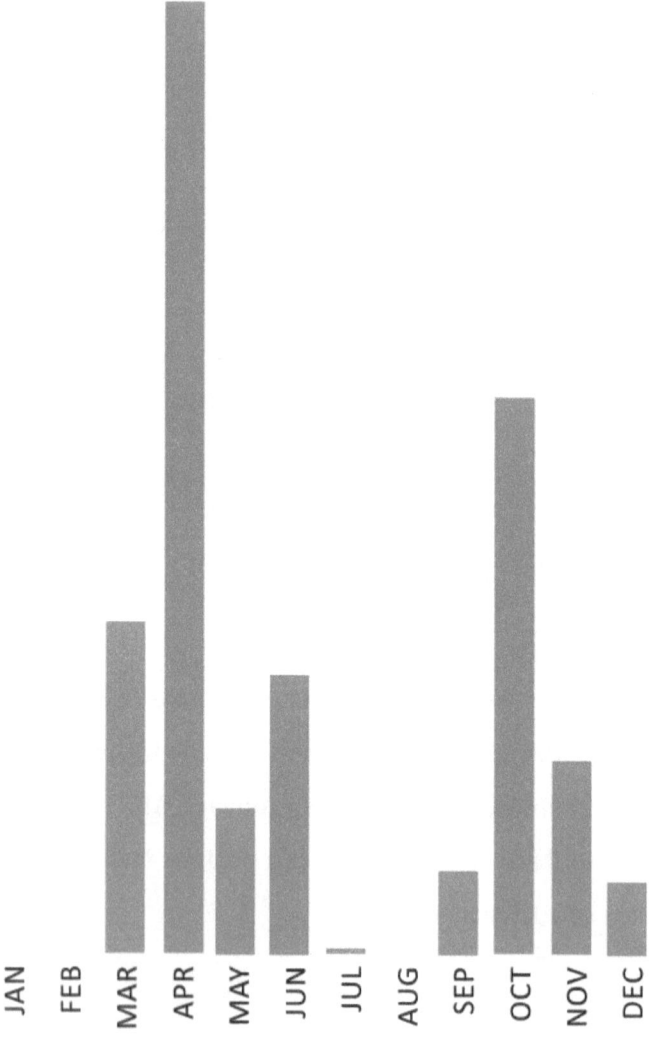

There was $67,073,604 worth of sales in 2019, with April and October seeing the highest sales totals. April was by far the most successful month with $24,073,625 realised from the combined totals of 6 photography sales.

The following shows the sales totals of each active month:

March: **$8,412,165**

April: **$24,073,625**

May: **$3,639,374**

June: **$7,982,836**

July: **$76,375**

October: **$14,059,189**

November: **$4,934,478**

December: **$1,700,000**

Sales total of all photography auctions: **$67,073,604**

The 50 Most Expensive Photographs
To Sell At Auction

The following data is gathered from results lists published by various auction houses. All results are in US dollars according to the exchange rate when results were published. All information correct at time of publication, December 2019.

50.

Joueur d'Orgue

Eugene Atget

Christie's New York, April 2010

$686,500

49.

Identical Twins, Roselle, N.J., 1966

Diane Arbus

Christie's New York, October 2018

$732,500

48.

Betty in her Attic, 1920

Edward Weston

Christie's New York, October 2017

$732,500

47.

Hong Kong, Stock Exchange (Diptych)

Andreas Gursky

Sotheby's London, June 2013

$783,225

46.

Freischwimmer 84

Wolfgang Tillmans

Phillips London, June 2017

$780,450

45.

Circus Tent

Edward Weston

Phillips New York, April 2019

$788,000

44.

The Great Wave, Sete

Gustave Le Gray

Sotheby's London, October 1999

$837,375

43.

Nude, 1925

Edward Weston

Christie's New York, April 2017

$871,500

42.

113 Athenes, Temple de Jupiter

Joseph Philibert Girault de Prangey

Christie's London, May 2003

$921,357

41.

Tokyo, Stock Exchange

Andreas Gursky

Sotheby's London, June 2013

$958,545

40.

Bateaux quittant le port du Havre
(navires de la flute de Napoleon III)

Gustave Le Gray

Christie's New York, February 2016

$965,000

39.

Panoramic Nude with Gun, Villa d'este,
Como, 1989

Helmut Newton

Phillips London, May 2018

$981,884

38.

May Day IV

Andreas Gursky

Christie's London, October 2017

$1,001,550

37.

Kuwait, Stock Exchange II

Andreas Gursky

Sotheby's London, June 2013

$1,013,625

36.

Nautilus

Edward Weston

Sotheby's New York, October 2007

$1,105,000

35.

Red Morning (Hell)

Gilbert & George

Christie's London, October 2017

$1,120,350

34.

Dovima with Elephant, Evening Dress by Dior, Cirque d'Hiver, Paris, 1955

Richard Avedon

Christie's Paris, November 2010

$1,143,760

33.

Self-Portrait ('The Constructor')

El Lissitzky

Christie's London, March 2019

$1,240,897

32.

Untitled (cowboy)

Richard Prince

Christie's New York, November 2005

$1,248,000

31.

Pantheon, Rome

Thomas Struth

Sotheby's London, June 2013

$1,252,305

30.

Georgia O'Keeffe - Nude

Alfred Stieglitz

Sotheby's New York, February 2006

$1,360,000

29.

Georgia O'Keeffe - Hands

Alfred Stieglitz

Sotheby's New York, February 2006

$1,470,000

28.

Untitled Film Still #48

Cindy Sherman

Sotheby's New York, April 2008

$1,565,000

27.

Nude 1925

Edward Weston

Sotheby's New York, April 2008

$1,609,000

26.

Shanghai 2000

Andreas Gursky

Sotheby's London, July 2015

$1,730,040

25.

Tobolsk Kremlin

Dimitry Medvedev

Christmas Yarmarka, Saint Petersburg, January 2010

$1,750,000

24.

Red Morning (Hate)

Gilbert & George

Christie's New York, November 2013

$1,805,000

23.

Pantheon, Rome

Thomas Struth

Sotheby's New York, May 2016

$1,810,000

22.

Sie Kommen, Paris (Dressed and Naked)

Helmut Newton

Phillips New York, April 2019

$1,820,000

21.

Rhein

Andreas Gursky

Phillips New York, May 2013

$1,925,000

20.

Untitled #92

Cindy Sherman

Christie's New York, November 2013

$2,045,000

19.

Portrait of a Tearful Woman

Man Ray

Christie's New York, May 2017

$2,167,500

18.

Untitled Film Still #48

Cindy Sherman

Sotheby's New York, November 2014

$2,225,000

17.

Billy The Kid

Unknown

Brian Lebel's Old West Show & Auction, June 2011

$2,300,000

16.

Chicago Board of Trade

Andreas Gursky

Sotheby's London, June 2013

$2,353,905

15.

Paris, Montparnasse

Andreas Gursky

Sotheby's London, October 2013

$2,386,825

14.

Untitled #153

Cindy Sherman

Phillips New York, November 2010

$2,770,500

13.

Untitled #96

Cindy Sherman

Christie's New York, May 2012

$2,882,500

12.

The Pond - Moonlight

Edward Steichen

Sotheby's New York, February 2006

$2,928,000

11.

Los Angeles

Andreas Gursky

Sotheby's London, February 2008

$2,938,235

10.

Untitled Film Still #48

Cindy Sherman

Christie's New York, May 2015

$2,965,000

9.

Untitled (cowboy)

Richard Prince

Sotheby's New York, May 2014

$3,077,000

8.

Noire et Blanche

Man Ray

Christie's Paris, November 2017

$3,118,950

7.

Chicago Board of Trade III

Andreas Gursky

Sotheby's London, June 2013

$3,296,385

6.

99 Cent II Diptychon

Andreas Gursky

Sotheby's London, February 2007

$3,332,000

5.

Dead Troops Talk

Jeff Wall

Christie's New York, May 2012

$3,666,500

4.

To Her Majesty

Gilbert & George

Christie's London, June 2008

$3,759,607

3.

Untitled #96

Cindy Sherman

Christie's New York, May 2011

$3,890,500

2.

Spiritual America

Richard Prince

Christie's New York, May 2014

$3,973,000

1.

Rhine II

Andreas Gursky

Christie's New York, November 2011

$4,338,500

Items of Interest in 2019

Sotheby's New York Expansion Completed

The galleries at Sotheby's New York headquarters on the Upper East Side were completed and revealed in May of 2019. The ambitious remodelling was designed by Shohei Shigematsu of the New York architectural firm OMA and saw the exhibition spaces increase in size from 67,000 square feet to 90,000 square feet. As well as exhibition and auction spaces the redesign also brings a new coffee bar, state-of-the-art reception and retail space. In all, Sotheby's NY now enjoys forty galleries including three two-storey spaces for large-scale works and a 150-foot long space. The unveiling coincided with Sotheby's *Impressionist & Modern* and *Contemporary Art* auctions at the height of what many reporters consider an overall art market downturn.

The Loss of Several Titans of Photography

Numerous stalwarts of photography passed away in 2019 including Terry O'Neil who died of Prostate Cancer at the age of 81. O'Neil was best known for his iconic images of 1960's London, with a portfolio of portraits including those of David Bowie, the Rolling Stones, Elton John and the Beatles. O'Neill's work was venerated with numerous exhibitions and publications to his name as well as an Honorary Fellowship of the Royal Photographic Society and a recently CBE for services to Photography.

Ormond Gigli, who was best known for his "Girls in the Windows" image, which routinely sells at auction, died at the latter end of 2019. It is believed Gigli passed away while at home in West Stockbridge, Massachusetts at the age of 94. The photographer's work appeared in publications such as Time, Life and Paris Match.

Perhaps the most talked-about death of the year was the passing of Peter Lindberg, largely credited as capturing the rise of the supermodel. Lindberg photographed icons such as Naomi Campbell and Cindy Crawford during a career that spanned four decades with his work appearing in magazines such as Vogue and Vanity Fair and exhibitions in galleries like the Gagosian and the Metropolitan Museum of Art. Lindberg died in Paris at the age of 74.

Sotheby's Goes Private

This year a huge shift occurred at Sotheby's when shareholders voted to approve an acquisition deal with the plan to go private before the end of the year.

In July of 2019 it was reported that three shareholders in Sotheby's had filed a lawsuit against the potential acquisition of the auction house by BidFair USA. The reasons given for the lawsuit included "incomplete and misleading disclosures about the deal". These lawsuits, however, do not seemed to have derailed the plans as 91% of Sotheby's shareholders went on to approve the deal in September.

The agreement valued the auction house at $3.7 billion and will take the company private for the first time since 1988 with shares valued at $57. Sotheby's transition into a private company will align the auction house with competitors Christie's and Phillips who also function as private companies.

French-Israeli Patrick Drahi who is founder and controlling shareholder of telecommunication company Altice is the owner of BidFair. Drahi is said to be an art collector himself and has an estimated personal networth of over $9 billion.

References

Items of Interest 2019

Armstrong, Annie. (2019) *Sotheby's Shareholders Vote to Approve Acquisition Deal, with Plan to Go Private by End of 2019* [online]. Art News. Available: https://www.artnews.com/art-news/news/sothebys-shareholders-patrick-drahi-13183/

BBC (2019) *Terry O'Neill: British Photographer To The Stars Dies Aged 81* [online]. Available: https://www.bbc.co.uk/news/uk-50452568

New York Times (2019) *Peter Lindbergh, Photographer Who Captured Rise of the Supermodel Dies at 74* [online]. Available: https://www.nytimes.com/2019/09/04/fashion/peter-lindbergh-dead.html

Sotheby's (2019) *Our New York Galleries, Expanded and Reimagined* [online]. Available: https://www.sothebys.com/en/articles/our-new-york-headquarters-expanded-and-reimagined

The Berkshire Edge (2019) *Ormond Gigli, 94, of West Stockbridge, photographer of 20th-century icons* [online]. Available: https://theberkshireedge.com/ormond-gigli-94-of-west-stockbridge-photographer-of-20th-century-icons/

Looking Back at Photography's Place at Auction in 2018

Arbus, D. (2018) *Photographs*. [online] Christie's, New York. Available: https://www.christies.com/lotfinder/Lot/diane-arbus-19231971-identical-twins-roselle-nj-6159681-details.aspx

Da Vinci, L. *Salvator Mundi*. (2017) *Post-War & Contemporary Art Evening Sale*. [online] Christie's, New York. Available: https://www.christies.com/lotfinder/Lot/leonardo-da-vinci-1452-1519-salvator-mundi-6110563-details.aspx

Gursky, A. *Rhine II*. (2011) *Post-War Contemporary Evening Sale*. [online] Christie's, New York. Available:

https://www.christies.com/lotfinder/Lot/andreas-gursky-b-1955-rhein-ii-5496716-details.aspx

Newton, H. *Panoramic Nude with Gun, Villa d'Este, Como* (2018) *Ultimate Evening & Photographs Day Sales*. [online] Phillips, London. Available:
https://www.phillips.com/detail/HELMUT-NEWTON/UK040118/16

Ray, M. *Noire et Blanche*. (2017) *Stripped Bare: Photographs from the Collection of Thomas Koerfer*. [online] Christie's, Paris. Available:
https://www.christies.com/lotfinder/Lot/man-ray-1890-1976-noire-et-blanche-1926-6105841-details.aspx

Fact Checking The Most Expensive Photographs Sold at Auction

Nuttal, F. (2018) *The Photography at Auction Digest, Volume One*. Amazon.

What The Winter Auctions Mean For Photography

PAA (2019) *What The Winter Auctions Mean For Photography*. [online] Photography at Auction. Available:
https://www.photographyatauction.com/what-the-winter-auctions-mean-for-photography/

How Photography is Performing at Auction [so far]

PAA (2019) *How Photography is Performing at Auction [so far]*. [online] Photography at Auction. Available:
https://www.photographyatauction.com/how-photography-is-performing-at-auction-so-far/

Photography's $67 Million Year

PAA (2019) *Photography's $67 Million Dollar Year.* [online] Photography at Auction. Available: https://www.photographyatauction.com/photographys-67-million-dollar-year

Further Reading

Christie's. (2019) *Photographs* [online]. Christie's. Available: https://www.christies.com/departments/Photographs-72-1.aspx

Phillips. (2019) *Photography Department* [online]. Phillips. Available: https://www.phillips.com/photographs

Sotheby's. (2019) *Photographs* [online]. Sotheby's. Available: https://www.sothebys.com/en/departments/photographs

Thank you for buying this book

Thank you for purchasing this book. Profits made from this sale contribute towards the ongoing upkeep of PhotographyAtAuction.com

Please review this book on Amazon

For more information on photography at auction, to see the photographs mentioned in this book, the results of auctions and other photography-related news visit www.photographyatauction.com

Other *Photography At Auction* books include:

The Photography at Auction Digest, Vol. I

Selling Your Work At Auction: A Roadmap To The Salesroom